St. Dunstan

Eliza Allen Starr

Kessinger Publishing's Rare Reprints

Thousands of Scarce and Hard-to-Find Books on These and other Subjects!

- Americana
- Ancient Mysteries
- Animals
- Anthropology
- Architecture
- Arts
- Astrology
- Bibliographies
- Biographies & Memoirs
- Body, Mind & Spirit
- Business & Investing
- Children & Young Adult
- Collectibles
- Comparative Religions
- Crafts & Hobbies
- Earth Sciences
- Education
- Ephemera
- Fiction
- Folklore
- Geography
- Health & Diet
- History
- Hobbies & Leisure
- Humor
- Illustrated Books
- Language & Culture
- Law
- Life Sciences

- Literature
- Medicine & Pharmacy
- Metaphysical
- Music
- Mystery & Crime
- Mythology
- Natural History
- Outdoor & Nature
- Philosophy
- Poetry
- Political Science
- Science
- Psychiatry & Psychology
- Reference
- Religion & Spiritualism
- Rhetoric
- Sacred Books
- Science Fiction
- Science & Technology
- Self-Help
- Social Sciences
- Symbolism
- Theatre & Drama
- Theology
- Travel & Explorations
- War & Military
- Women
- Yoga
- *Plus Much More!*

We kindly invite you to view our catalog list at:
http://www.kessinger.net

SAINT DUNSTAN.

MONG the illustrated books that were the delight of my childhood, was one containing a picture of St. Dunstan, archbishop of Canterbury and primate of the Church in England. He was represented as of most venerable aspect, and writing with a style, or ancient pen. An account of this great man's life was also given with the picture; and besides the praise given to his fervent piety, his profound learning, his prudence and holy wisdom, he was said to have been an illuminator, as well as an accomplished transcriber or copyist, of sacred books. The volume containing all this was not a Catholic one, merely a popular magazine for children, scattered all over New England. I have often wondered if the other children in the neighborhood liked this picture as well as I did; if they remembered it; and if it was to them, as to me, a point of attraction, around which gathered, in after years, noble traditions and generous sentiments.

St. Dunstan was a native of Glastonbury, "That holiest spot," it has been said, "in all England;" for there the faith was first planted by a person no less honorable than St. Joseph of Arimathea, that "rich man" and "noble counsellor," as he is called in the gospels, who assisted with his devout hands to take down the body of his Divine Lord from the cross, and, wrapping it in fine linen and the most costly spices, laid it in his own new tomb. Thirty years after he had earned, by this act of love, a place in the heart of every Christian, flying from the persecutions of his countrymen and taking with him, as his only treasure, a few drops of the Blood of his Redeemer, he landed on the western shore of England and found a peaceful asylum on an island surrounded by marshes. This island was called by the Britons, Avallona, or Isle-of-apples, because it abounded with apple-trees; and we are told that every year the island still blushes with the delicate bloom of its orchards. It is from the Britons themselves that we inherit the tradition of the landing of St. Joseph of Arimathea with his twelve companions; and of the drops of Precious Blood that he brought with him, preserved in the same chalice that was used by Jesus Christ at the Last Supper, when he instituted the Holy Eucharist. This tradition of the chalice and its sacred contents, was kept alive in those poems celebrating the virtues of the " Knights of the Round Table " in King Arthur's time, all of whom ardently desired to possess this holy relic, called the *Saint Graal,* or "Holy Cup." To the

16

Britons themselves, also, we trace back the lovely legend of the first miracle on British soil, performed by St. Joseph of Arimathea to save the souls of a few simple-minded savages, and thus laying deep in the national heart the seed of Christian faith which he had come to plant on that distant shore. Received with kindness by the Britons, he chose the first moment in which he saw them hesitating to believe what he was telling them of Christ and his religion, to confirm their faith by a miracle. Planting his pilgrim staff, cut from the same thorn tree of Palestine from which the Roman soldiers had gathered the thorns that crowned the head of Jesus in His sorrowful passion, into the unblessed, pagan soil, lo! the dry staff quickened at the prayer of this lover of souls, and sent forth leaf-buds into the cold December air; at sight of which the poor pagans fell at the feet of the messenger of the Prince of Peace, and were converted, listening with docility to the word he had come to preach to them. And not only did the thorn send out its tender leaf-buds, but it struck roots, strong and healthy roots, into the fresh British soil, blossoming, during fifteen hundred years, for the edification of the faithful, and is still to be seen by the pilgrim to the shrine of Glastonbury. Here, too, this same Joseph of Arimathea built a chapel out of the twisted and interlaced branches of the willow, and consecrated it to the Blessed Virgin; that Mother of Sorrows, to whose supernatural grief and supernatural fortitude he was an eye-witness, and which he must have carried in his memory, as a fountain of devotion, to his death.

Such was the beginning of the great abbey of Glastonbury; and tradition tells us that within its walls lies the dust of that spotless Christian knight, King Arthur; for, having been mortally wounded in one of those long battles between the Britons and their Saxon invaders which lasted three days and nights, he was carried to the good and faithful monks at Glastonbury, died with them, and was there secretly buried.

At Glastonbury, then, we might look for a saint; and it was in this old Christian town, sanctified by such precious memories, that St. Dunstan was born. The exact date of his birth does not seem to be known, but it was probably before 940, or in that tenth century, which has been called the darkest century of the Christian Church. Here, then, at Glastonbury, he was offered by his parents at the altar of Our Lady, and as soon as he could prattle was given over by them to the care of some Irish monks who settled in the deserted abbey, earning the bare nesessaries of life by teaching the children of the neighborhood. Of these good monks he learned the doctrines of the Christian Church, and also the elements of sound scholarship. Centuries before the time of St. Dunstan there was a great school at Glastonbury. Students from Ireland and Scotland and France, as well as from England itself, came to Glastonbury to drink at its full fountain of learning. But Glastonbury had shared the fate of many other noble retreats for learning and piety during the invasions of the barbarians from the north of Europe; and what, in the time of Venerable Bede, as you have already seen in his life, was a centre of civilization and learning, being under the protection of a great religious community, was, at the time of St. Dunstan's birth, a melancholy home for a few monks, who showed their love for learning by teaching it to the young children around them. Most happy, however, were those "excellent masters of the sciences," those few monks at Glastonbury, for to them the providence of God committed the training of one of His noblest saints on the list of the British Isles. His extraordinary genius soon showed itself, and he outstripped his companions in every branch of study which had any interest for him. Thus accomplished in the learning of his age, and enjoying the advantages of his noble birth, he was taken to the court of the good king, Athelstan, by his uncle, Athelmus, archbishop of Canterbury. Athelstan, who was a lover of virtue and of learning, honored Dunstan with a regard above that which he gave to any other person at the court, which so excited the envy and jealousy of the ambitious courtiers that they did not hesitate to invent all sorts of malicious lies, charging Dunstan, even to the king, with the practice of sorcery; a foolish story founded upon his musical skill, by which he was said to bewitch the king; and they also accused him of a heathenish regard for the poetry of the old Saxon bards. After a short struggle to keep his high place at court against such enemies, he retired to the house of his relative, the bishop of Winchester. Here he had leisure to meditate upon the fleeting honors of a life in the world, and to lay out a holy plan for the future. The good providence of God did not forsake him under these misfortunes. His life had been one of singular devotion and purity, and although he was not willing to be driven from an honorable place near the king, to which his birth, his genius, and his learning gave him a just claim, he was far from any worldly habit of mind. While in these good dispositions a long and severe illness showed to him, as nothing else can, the nothingness of all earthly goods compared with heavenly ones; and on his recovery he offered himself to the bishop for the service of God. The habit of a monk in the order of priesthood was given to him, and he was sent to the very church in which he was baptized, and to the abbey where he had lived, as a child and a youth, with his old friends, the learned Irish monks of Glastonbury.

Before he left this school of religion and of letters, of science and of art, his skill in music, painting, engraving and working in metals, had won for him a wide-spread and just fame. Some of my readers may be surprised that a young man in the "Dark Ages," should have been encouraged to aspire to such a varied and noble culture, especially as he did not appear to have a vocation for a priestly or monastic life. We often hear people saying, that in those ages none but priests were allowed to be scholars; yet here is a young and elegant courtier coveting every accomplish-

ment that could grace his rank at the present day. It
was after he had learned, at the court of the good
king, Athelstan, that "all is vanity" outside the service of God—which indeed none learn so well as
those who have had enough of the pleasures and
grandeurs of the world to know how hollow are all
the appearances of such happiness, how far short of
the desires of the human heart are all the contrivances
of society for enjoyment—that Dunstan was ready to
bring to the service of God, and to the service of the
Church, the treasures he had received from his pious
instructors. ·In the retirement of his monastic life at
Glastonbury, we find him embellishing the Sacred
Books with all the zeal, and patience, and industry,
peculiar to the student-monk and ecclesiastic, of that
period. He could, without wrong to any one, apply
himself to the studies he so much loved, and to that
art of the illuminator which was then devoted, in all
its freshness and pefection, to the beautifying of the
sacred text. The canonical books of the Bible, were,
in those ages, laboriously written out by hand on vel-
lum or parchment. The work of a copyist was con-
sidered a very responsible one, as the correctness of
the sacred text was so easily impaired. To copy, per-
fectly, was a great merit; but, in addition to this, to
design, and execute in the most brilliant and lasting
colors, pictures illustrating the great events in the Old
or New Testaments, was, in those ages of faith, looked
upon as a labor receiving the choicest blessing of
Heaven as its great, its only reward. At the present

time, there is a general turning of amateur pencils and brushes to the imitating of these beautiful remains of the devotional art of the middle ages; but these feeble attempts have not the aim of those good monks to inspire them. Much as the nineteenth century boasts of its love for the Bible, it has never produced such decorations for the holy text as were executed, under the greatest inconveniences, by a set of men, whom the Reformation has branded as "ignorant of the Bible." Many of these mediæval artists were simple monks, peaceful, patient, laborious; but besides these, (who have not left an initial letter by which their works might be known, much less their names remembered), we find that more than one bishop of the Church was honored, as an illuminator of Scripture. In every convent were skillful masters of the pen and pencil, and a copy of the gospels is still preserved in the British Museum, with an inscription, telling us that it was "written by the hands of Eadfrith, that Bishop Ethelwald added the illuminations, whilst Bilfrid, the ankret, bound it in sheets of silver-gilt, and set it with jewels, and the priest Alfrid furnished the Anglo-Saxon Gloss" (*i. e.*, explanations or comments). As I have said, Dunstan, the profound scholar, the holy ecclesiastic, the companion of princes, the favorite of a good and learned king, had this praise added to the list of his many virtues, that he "*excelled* in illumination." In a manuscript in the Oxford Library there is a drawing from his hand, a figure of Jesus Christ appearing to Dunstan who is adoring at his feet. So

enthusiastic was the regard entertained for these works
of the devout illuminators, that, after death, the right
hand which had wrought such glowing devices to
illustrate the Word of God was often carefully em-
balmed.

But not in painting, alone, was Dunstan famous
as an artist; he was also skilled in the working of
precious metals for the sacred vessels, in designing
embroideries for chasubles, and even in the casting of
bells. In reading the delightful annals of that century
—delightful in spite of many sorrowful irregularities,
since faith was still recognized and still lived out by
Christians in all parts of Europe,—we often come upon
passages that tell us of the priestly gifts of exquisitely
wrought gold and silver altar ornaments, sent by
Dunstan as the work of his own hands to some mis-
sionary friend in a wild country. It is said, that of
the four large bells that afterwards adorned the new
abbey church at Abingdon, two were cast by the hands
of the abbot, and two, yet larger ones, were the handi-
work of St. Dunstan. It was one of his delights, also,
to carve in wood, to mould figures in clay and wax,
and to engrave. Mention is made of a vestment em-
broiderd by a royal lady, Ethelfreda, for which St.
Dunstan made the design. Indeed the art of designing, as well as the labor of the artistic workman, was
encouraged in those ages with priests and monks of
all ranks, as it gave them the recreation which every
one needs, and also saved them from the dangers of
idleness.

In these peaceful and holy labors Dunstan passed his monastic life at Glastonbury, when the death of King Athelstan, and the coming to the throne of his brother Edmund, again drew him from his seclusion. Edmund's palace of Chedder was only nine miles from Glastonbury, and he often visited its old church with singular devotion. In this way he became acquainted with the sanctity of St. Dunstan, and, calling him back to the court, made him his chief counsellor, and gave him the territory of Glastonbury that he might be able to restore the abbey to its former splendor. Dunstan immediately collected a community, giving it the rule of St. Benedict; and, in doing this, he became the restorer of order, and the reviver of learning, in his native country.

Nothing could exceed the prudent zeal with which Dunstan brought back among the people the schools that had been destroyed by public calamities, and revived the seminaries for the education of priests in the new abbeys, springing up under his wise and vigorous government; and in these schools and seminaries some of the most famous ecclesiastics of that century received their education. St. Dunstan allowed the reading of the Latin poets, because, as he said, it polished the mind and improved the style; he also encouraged the study of Anglo-Saxon poetry, that his preachers might speak, eloquently, their native tongue. Science was not forgotten, and arithmetic, geometry, astronomy, and music were carefully cultivated by his pupils, while many of them excelled in the art of painting, so especially beloved by their master. In the time of good King Alfred, who mourned over the low state of knowledge in his age, monks were despised, and few but ignorant and rude persons could be persuaded to wear a cowl. St. Dunstan turned the tide, and Glastonbury could soon found other houses and other schools from the ranks of its own well taught scholars. Among these scholars was Ethelwold, whose name is found, so often and so pleasantly, on the same page with St. Dunstan's, that we never see one without expecting to see the other. Ethelwold, too, was the abbot whose bells chimed in so sweetly with the bells of St. Dunstan from the towers of the new abbey. One of the graces for which the writers of that age tell us he was distinguished, was a peculiar charm of manner that drew to him the hearts of the young. To any one who is devoting a lifetime to the instruction of youth, nothing can be more gratifying than the honor and love manifested towards their teachers by the young of those distant, and (as we are so apt to believe) rude, times.

King Edmund reigned but six years and a half, and his two sons, Edwy and Edgar, being too young to govern, his nephew Edred was called to the throne, and his veneration for St. Dunstan was even greater than the veneration of his uncle, Edmund. To Edred succeeded the unworthy Edwy, a profligate youth, who on the very day of his coronation insulted the noble guests at his table. It was the courageous reproof given to him on that day by his royal father's old counsellor and dear friend, St. Dunstan, which the wicked Edwy could never forgive. St. Dunstan was obliged to escape to Flanders, and the two abbeys of Glastonbury and Abingdon, governed by Dunstan, were broken up, and the monks scattered by the order of the king. But his exile only served to spread abroad the sweet odor of his sanctity. At the church of St. Peter's, at Ghent, a vestment is still shown that was worn by St. Dunstan. As to Edwy, his people soon threw off the hateful hand of the tyrant, and set upon the throne his brother Edgar, who immediately called home our saint and promoted him to the same post of confidence that he had filled under his father and his uncle. He was soon made bishop of Worcester; two years later he was made primate, and going to Rome to receive the Pallium,* was sent home to England as the Apostolic Legate.

He was now in a position to carry out all his noble plans for the reformation of abuses, and the establishment of schools and seminaries. Everywhere new monasteries were springing up; the old abbeys of Ely, Peterborough, Malmsbury and Thorney, rose out of their ruins; and such was the eagerness of the king and of his people, that more than forty abbeys were founded or restored while St. Dunstan was primate. Can you believe that we are talking about a saint in the "Dark Ages?"

Besides these grand and imposing works he revived

---

* See *Pallium* in the life of St. Agnes.

the parochial schools, required the priests to preach every Sunday to their flocks, and, in their schools, to teach their parish children grammar, the church-chant, and some useful trade. Do you think, my dear young readers, that these "Middle Age" children under the protection of the good primate, St. Dunstan, need much pity even from the children of the present day and in the United States?

It was during the life of St. Dunstan that the wishes of the good king, Alfred, or Alfred the Great as he is called, were really carried out, for in St. Dunstan's time, under his encouragement and that of his friend Ethelwold, everything was done to instruct the people in their own language. Besides translating several of the books of Scripture, Ælfric, one of Ethelwold's scholars, devoted to English literature, composed a Latin and English grammar, and other school-books, for the use of beginners. I cannot so much as name all the good works, to encourage learning and solid piety, performed, or inspired, by St. Dunstan. Good schools arose in every part of the kingdom, and the annals of Ramsey Abbey would interest my youngest reader, or—listener; for, many a little boy and girl who cannot yet read fast enough to read these pages for themselves, will, I hope, hear them read by some older child in the family. One pretty incident may touch the fancy of some good-hearted little rogue who is perhaps charged with all the mischief done in the house, and, sometimes is told that he is the naughtiest boy in the world and that every body despairs of him.

If such a little boy gets hold of this book let him read for his comfort about four little fellows in the school of Ramsey Abbey.

"Four little boys, named Oswald, Etheric, Ædnoth and Athelstan, had been placed in the school by St. Oswald (a dear friend of St. Dunstan's), all being sons of powerful Saxon *thanes*, or lords. They were received before they were seven years old, and were of innocent manners and beautiful countenances. At certain times they were suffered by their master to go and play outside the cloister walls. One day, being thus sent out by themselves, they ran to the great west tower, and laying hold of the bell-rope, rang with all their might, but so unskilfully that one of the bells was cracked by the unusual motion. The mischief becoming known, the culprits were threatened with a sound flogging; a threat which occasioned abundance of tears. At last, remembering the sentence they had so often heard read from the rule of St. Benedict, 'If any one shall lose or break anything, let him hasten without delay to accuse himself of it,' they ran to the abbot, and, weeping bitterly, told him all that had happened. The good abbot pitied their distress, and calling the brethren together who were disposed to treat the matter rather severely, he said to them, 'These little innocents have committed a fault, but with no evil intention; they ought, therefore, to be spared, and when they grow up to be men it will be easy for them to make good the damage they have done.' Then dismissing the monks, he secretly ad-

13   17

monished the boys how to disarm their anger; and they, following his directions, entered the church with bare feet, and there made their vow; and when they grew up to manhood and were raised to wealth and honor, they remembered what they had promised, and bestowed great benefits on the Church."

No doubt my little friends have often been told not to conceal any mischief they may have done, however grave, or, however unintentional; but they may not have supposed that St. Benedict would provide for accidents in a rule for monasteries. I hope the knowing this, and the success of the four little boys in the old abbey of Ramsey in escaping a whipping by obeying this rule, will fix it so tightly in the memory of every child who hears about it, that none of you will ever fail to accuse yourselves of all your mischief, and bear, bravely, your punishment, if you cannot get rid of it, rather than be a skulking coward of a child, to grow up into a mean, cowardly man, or a deceitful, cowardly woman, ready to tell all sorts of lies in order to cover up a poor little mistake, as well as some great blunder. Own up to all your mistakes and blunders, but never be a coward and, almost of course, a liar. I shudder when I remember all the misery, injustice, and heart-break, that has come on families, neighborhoods, and countries, by some cowardly act to save one's self from deserved blame. One hardly knows whether most to pity or to despise the person who can allow another, innocent, person, to suffer for his sin or his blunder. Of one thing, however, I am certain; St. Benedict pitied and despised such conduct as much as we possibly can, or he would never have made that splendid rule, "*Make haste* to accuse yourself if you have lost or have broken anything." Remember this as long as you live, and act upon it, and you will not suffer in purgatory for some mean sin of concealment, that perhaps seemed small, but which drew after it such consequences as make death-beds hard. Be good, courageous, noble-hearted Christian boys and girls, if you expect to look our dear Lord full in the face at your private, individual judgment; and though you may be obliged to stay awhile in purgatory, you will remember, all through its great pains, the dear, dear look in the eyes of your kind Judge, who hated lies and told who was the father of them.

You have, no doubt, conceived a high regard for King Edgar, under whose powerful protection St. Dunstan performed such prodigies of goodness and wisdom. I must now tell you of a great misfortune that befell Edgar. You may fancy that I shall tell you that an army of barbarians invaded his kingdom; or that some one of his household was treacherous; or that he lost his children. Any, or all, of these dreadful misfortunes might have come upon Edgar and it would not have been so terrible as this one— for he was so unfortunate as to fall into a terrible sin. I say, he was so unfortunate; because we cannot suppose that Edgar intended to commit such a crime, until his passions had blinded him to its enormity. In those early days of Christian civilization there were fewer social restraints upon the untamed passions of men, and especially of kings, than at present, when the laws of the land and of society have all been modeled, for many centuries, on the principles of Christian morality. Therefore the Christians of those days, and especially the kings, were more in danger of surprises, and were more exposed to falling into scandalous sins. King Edgar, then, as I have said, was surprised by a great temptation and he yielded to it. St. Dunstan immediately sought him out, and, with all the boldness of the prophet Nathan before King David, he remonstrated with him on his sin. The king, struck with remorse, begged, with many tears, that a suitable penance might be laid upon him, and St. Dunstan gave him a penance for seven years. During this time he was never to wear his crown, was to fast twice every week, and give large alms. He was also bound to build an extensive nunnery, in which Christian virgins might be consecrated to the service of God. These conditions the king faithfully kept, and founded a rich convent for nuns at Shaftsbury. When the seven years of his penance were over, St. Dunstan, in a public assembly of the lords and prelates, set the crown again upon his head, and thus gave, to the entire kingdom, an example against sin in high places.

We know that many persons, in this age of the world, would prefer to have a wicked king or ruler go on committing wickedness, to allowing the priests and bishops of the Church to have so great an influence over him. But in England at that time all were glad that there was a spiritual power respected even by kings, and we, certainly, need not wish that Edgar had despised St. Dunstan or his counsels.

Notwithstanding the great labors connected with such a life as that of the holy archbishop of Canterbury, we read that he frequently visited the churches in all parts of the kingdom. Those who live in large cities, surrounded by the luxuries of religion, often forget the privations and irregularities suffered by those who live in some far off corner of a diocese or province; and also forget the pleasure felt by the pastors and inhabitants, of these lonely districts, when they find themselves, and their interests, affectionately remembered by their superiors. It puts new heart and life into their labors, and they meet with courage, after such a visit, what before overwhelmed them. On these pastoral visits St. Dunstan preached often and with great eloquence; and few were so hardened as to resist his appeals. He employed all his revenues for the relief of the poor, and no heart in all England was more tender towards the suffering than that of its great primate. But neither the care of the churches, the monasteries, the schools, nor the attendance upon the king, nor even the necessities of the poor, ever made him neglect his prayers and meditations; and after the occupations of his crowded day were over, he watched late into the night in communion with God. Glastonbury was his dearest solitude, and thither he would often retire from the world to give himself up to heavenly contemplation.　When at Canterbury it was his custom, even in the coldest weather, to visit the church of St. Austin (or St. Augustine, apostle of England), outside the walls, and that of the Blessed Virgin adjoining it.

We must now see how this good man died.　'In 988 St. Dunstan had grown very feeble, and the feast of the Ascension in that year was the last day on which his voice was heard in the solemnities of his cathedral.　On that day, after the reading of the gospel, he walked in state from the vestry to the pulpit, and preached with surpassing energy on the Incarnation of Jesus Christ, the redemption of man and the bliss of heaven.　He then went on with the mass until the end of the *Pater Noster* when he again turned to his people, exhorting them to follow their head and leader to the realms of happiness, and pronounced over them the episcopal benediction.　After the kiss of peace he addressed them a third time, as if his heart yearned towards them, and begged them to remember him when he was gone; for he felt that his hour of death was very near, and that he should see them no more in this world.　The tears of the clergy and of the people proved their affection for this venerable saint, to whom they all owed so much.　He concluded the mass and had sufficient strength to take his usual place at the table in the hall for the festal banquet. After dinner he returned to the church, pointed out the spot in which he was to be buried, and then withdrew to his chamber, where he spent that day and the next in acts of devotion, and in advising and consoling those who visited him. On the Saturday after the Ascension, mass was celebrated in his room by his own order, and as soon as he had received the communion he burst into the following prayer: "Glory be to thee, Almighty Father, that hast given the bread of life from heaven to those who fear thee; that we may be mindful of thy wonderful mercy to man in the Incarnation of thine only-begotten Son, born of the Virgin. To thee Holy Father, for that when we were not thou didst give to us a being, and when we were sinners didst grant to us a Redeemer, we give due thanks through the same thy Son, our Lord and God, who, with thee and the Holy Ghost, maketh all things, governeth all things, and liveth through ages and ages, without end." Soon after this, on the 19th of May, the day on which the Church still honors him in her office, he calmly expired, it being the sixty-fourth, or the sixty-fifth, year of his age, and the twenty-seventh of his life as archbishop.' He was buried in his own cathedral, in the place he had appointed, though it is probable that some part of his relics were taken to his beloved Glastonbury.

In St. Dunstan we see the model of a monk, priest, bishop. The goods of this world, which he always possessed in abundance, were used for the highest and noblest interests of the Church, of God, and of the laity who make up so large a part of that Church. Our Lord said, "He that would be greatest among you let him be the servant of all;" and it was by his

right royal service towards the necessities of the Church
and the people, that St. Dunstan became "a great
priest, who in his day served God, and none was found
like to him who kept the law of the Most High."

Let us then invoke, with deep devotion, the revered
name of that saint whose holy life we have been
following, saying with humility, " Pray for us, holy
St. Dunstan, that we may be made worthy of the
promises of Christ;" that we too may be faithful servants in our day and generation and win, by that
service, the "Well done, good and faithful servant."
Then, my dear children, whether, as the years go on,
you belong to the flocks, or to the pastors, or to the
bishops, of the Church of God, whatever afflictions or
disappointments may await you here, you may be sure
of a crown of glory and the everlasting peace of the
faithful servants of God, and of His Church.

THE BELLS OF ABINGDON.

Ting—ting—yet never a tinkle;
　Ring—ring—yet never a sound
Stirs the beds of periwinkle,
　Stirs the ivy climbing round
The belfry-tower of well-hewn stone,
Where, ages ago, at Abingdon,

Saint Dunstan's bells, with Saint Ethelwold's hung;
    Hung and swung;
    Swung and rung;
        Rung,
Each with its marvellous choral tongue,
Matins and Lauds, and the hour of Prime,
Terce, Sext, and None, till the Vesper hymn
Was heard from the monks in their stalls so dim;
        Then lent their chime
To the solemn chorus of Compline time.
And blessed was he, or yeoman or lord,
Who, with stout bow armed or with goodly sword,
        Heard, at the hour,
Those wonderful bells of sweetness and power;
And, crossing himself with the sign of peace,
Had his Pater and Ave said at their cease.

Ting—ting—yet never a tinkle;
    Ring—ring—yet never a sound
Stirs the beds of periwinkle,
    Stirs the ivy creeping round,
Creeping, creeping, over the ground,
        As if to hide
From the eye of man his own rapine and pride.
Matins, and Lauds, and the hour of Prime;
Terce, Sext, None, Vespers, and Compline time,
        Unrung,
        Unsung;
    The bells and the friars
Alike in their graves; and the tangled briers

Bud in May, blush with blossoms in June,
Where the bells, that once were all in tune,
    Moulder beneath the ivy vines;
    Only, as summer day declines,
      The peasants hear,
      With pious fear,
Ting—ting—yet never a tinkle,
  Ring—ring—yet never a sound,
Where, in their beds of periwinkle,
  And ivy close to the ground,
Saint Dunstan's bells, with Saint Ethelwold's, keep
A silent tongue while the good monks sleep.